# A Path Worth Walking

## Finding True Intimacy with Jesus

Julie Collins

Printed in the United States of America


ISBN: 979-8-9858200-5-8


[Unless otherwise marked, all verses come from the NIV] THE HOLY
BIBLE, NEW INTERNATIONAL VERSION®, NIV®
Copyright © 1973, 1978, 1984, 2011 by Biblica, Inc.® Used by
permission. All rights reserved worldwide.

www.dowellhousepublishing.com

TABLE OF CONTENTS

# Dedication

This book is dedicated to my husband, Matt, for walking this path with me step-by-step as the Lord has led us. He is truly my hero in the faith.

# Week One

~

## Establishing That Intimacy

# Day One

## Are You His?

This week, we are going to make sure that we know we are born again and that Christ is our first love. We are going to learn how to talk to the Lord so we can grow in our intimacy with Him and learn how to hear from Him when He speaks.

**Start With Prayer**

Before we delve into the scriptures, it is so important to start with prayer because it is God's word and who better to explain to us what it means than the person who said it? If you haven't prayed before, please feel free to use the prayer below as a guide. Remember, you are talking to someone who loves you very much and wants to hear from you.

*"Lord, I want to thank you and praise you for being such a relational God and giving us your Word, the Bible, so we can learn, grow, and be spoken to. I pray that you will open my heart and mind to show me what I need to hear and see in your Word today. Give me wisdom and discernment as I read your living and Holy Word. I also pray that you will show me any areas in my life that I may have public or hidden sin. I want to ask for forgiveness and repent from my sinful ways. Lord, I love you and praise you. In your holy name I pray, amen."*

**Read: John 3:1-18**

The Pharisees were a Jewish sect that used God's law and their culture's traditions in their teaching. They were middle-class businessmen, merchants, and tradesmen. There were about six thousand of them during the time of Jesus. In John chapter three,

Jesus has an encounter with a Pharisee named Nicodemus. He came to see Jesus at night.

**Why do you think Nicodemus came to Jesus at night in verse 2?**

_____

_____

_____

_____

Many scholars have speculated why Nicodemus wanted to visit Jesus at night. It could have been because he didn't want anyone to see him and think he directly approved of Jesus' teaching. It could also have been the only time he could catch Jesus alone since crowds were following him during the day. Seeing the crowds of people following Jesus and the miracles he was performing most likely prompted Nicodemus to figure out who exactly this Jesus was.

**What did Nicodemus call Jesus in verse 2?**

_____

_____

_____

_____

He called him a "Rabbi." In Judaism, this is a religious teacher and spiritual mentor. Nicodemus, being a Pharisee and religious teacher at the time, would have also been called Rabbi. By calling Jesus, "Rabbi", he was putting himself in the humble role of the student again.

**What do you think Jesus meant when he said, "you must be born again" in verse 3?**

_____

_____

_____

_____

Nicodemus did not understand Jesus about being "born again". It didn't make any sense. No physical sense anyway. But, spiritually he knew he was not "born again". He had been doing things the same way his whole life and trying to earn his way to heaven by obeying God's Law.

I have known so many people, pastors, pastor's wives, missionaries included, who have been to church and heard God's Law their whole lives but didn't realize until later in life that they were NOT born again. But what does that mean exactly?

**What are some ways that people think they can get to Heaven?**

_____

_____

_____

_____

The Pharisees were the Rabbis, religious leaders, in Jesus' day. They were very strict about following the law. They held the law of God so highly that they made extra rules to make sure that people didn't even come close to breaking God's law because that is how they thought they were right with God. Nicodemus had spent his whole life in that strict culture where he received his religious education. Was following the law the only way to be clean before God? Still, something was missing and Nicodemus recognized that."

**What did Jesus say was missing?**

_____

_____

_____

_____

Do you remember the moment you got married or the moment you gave birth? Moments like these are one's you will never forget. You might not remember the date or the time but you knew that in those moments your life changed forever. The same way, you will remember the moment that you enter into a relationship with God. A relationship beyond just doing what you were supposed to do like going to church when the doors were open, trying to be a good person, trying to obey God's law, etc. It's the moment that you were spiritually reborn into the kingdom of God. I promise you will remember that moment for the rest of your life. Let me share with you the moment that I was born again.

I will always remember the moment that I was born again. When I was ten years old, my parents took us to the beautiful island of Hawaii for vacation. On Sunday, they took us to the church where they were members of a church a decade before, when they lived there. At the end of the church service during the invitation, I felt this overwhelming tug at my heart. I knew that I needed to walk the aisle to give my life to Christ.

The fear of walking to the front of that church in front of all those strangers was real and overwhelming, but the fear of the Lord was stronger. I tried to get to my mom so she could walk with me, but my brother, who was sitting right next to me, stuck his leg up so I couldn't get through. There is no doubt now that Satan was placing roadblocks in my way to keep me from that altar, but the draw of my Savior was strong. I grabbed my dad's hand who was sitting right by me, because I couldn't reach my mom and he walked down the aisle with me. When I reached the front, I talked to the pastor and surrendered my being, my soul, and my life to Christ. I remember feeling so clean and could not wait to tell everyone when I got back home to Tennessee.

**According to Jesus, what is the only way that we can get to Heaven? (verses 5-10)**

_____

_____

_____

_____

_____

**I want you to write John 3:16 below.**

_____

_____

_____

_____

**Who is salvation for and do I need it?**

_____

_____

_____

_____

I want you to truly understand what it means to be born again and why God had to send His only son Jesus to pay for our sins.

When God created the world, it was beautiful and sinless. Sin entered the world when the first man and women, Adam and Eve, chose to sin. That sin separated all of us from God. It would take a blood sacrifice to atone for their sins. Before Jesus came the people sacrificed animals to God to cover their sins. They had faith that one day God would fulfill His promise of sending a Messiah to finally deal with Satan and cover their sins once and for all.

When God sent His only son, Jesus, he paid the highest price to save man from their sins. God came down from His throne in the form of a man, Jesus, and lived an obedient and sinless life. He died on a cross to be the ultimate and final sacrifice to cover ALL the human race's sins. He rose from the grave three days later and now reigns in Heaven seated at the right hand of God.

It is not just an intellectual agreement that you believe Jesus is God. To truly build a relationship with him, we need to come to Him with a humble heart knowing that we are sinners and in need of His forgiveness. We must also believe that he truly is the son of

God, and that we can confidently put our trust in Him alone to cleanse of our sins and save us. We give Him our lives to follow and obey Him and He will change us to be more like Himself as we go.

I just really want you to understand and truly know that you are born again or you will not be able to experience the deep intimacy that I will be talking about in this book. Not only that, but you will not be able to enter into God's Kingdom if you are not one of His own as described above.

**Look at verses 17 and 18. What happens to the ones who do not believe?**

_____

_____

_____

_____

Before we move on into this study I want you to think back to the time you were born again into God's family. Take some time to reflect on your salvation. Do you remember the moment that you became His?

**Write a little bit of your story below. Share your experience with a friend.**

_____

_____

_____

_____

_____

_____

_____

_____

_____

_____

Romans 10: 9-10 says, *"If you declare with your mouth, "Jesus is Lord," and believe in your heart that God raised him from the dead, you will be saved. For it is with your heart that you believe and are justified, and it is with your mouth that you profess your faith and are saved.*

# Day Two
## Removing Idols

**Start with Prayer**

Ask the Lord to help you understand where you may have placed things before Him in your life.

**Read: Exodus 20: 1-6**

Establishing intimacy in a new relationship takes work, but it is even more difficult in the later years of a relationship when the honeymoon flame has seemingly gone out. The same can be true for our relationship with the Lord. It is important that we get back to him as our first love and remember how he became our love in the first place.

Today's passage picks up after God in his love rescued the Israelites out of bondage and slavery in Egypt. Egypt was a land of many idols and the belief in many gods. Each god represented a different aspect of life and it was common for the Egyptian people to worship a number of gods. They did this to make the gods happy in order to receive the maximum number of blessings and benefits.

In Exodus 12:40, the Bible says it has been 430 years since Joseph had brought his father Jacob and their family to the land of Egypt to escape the famine that decimated their home. The generations of Israelites living there would have been brought up in Egyptian culture and their religious traditions, more than likely, would have interwoven with their own verbal stories of the God of Abraham, Isaac and Jacob. There was nothing written about the one true God, yet there was so much recorded through writing and oral tradition of Egyptian culture regarding their false gods. Even though the Israelites were in slavery to the Egyptians, I imagine the religion still had a tight hold on them.

Now, in Exodus 20:1-6 the Israelites had been rescued through Moses by the hand of God and they were camped in the wilderness outside of Egypt, at the foot of Mt. Sinai. Again, through Moses, his servant, God was beginning to reveal Himself fully to his people. He wanted them to know what it was like to live in His family which looked drastically different then the Egyptian and the other surrounding cultures.

In verse 3, God made the first rule to his people, "You shall have no other gods before me." An "idol" or "god" is anything that is put in priority over and above the one true God, Yahweh. This could be your spouse, children, sports, money, yourself, pleasure, job, time, power, comfort, etc.

**Think about these things and list what you may be making a priority in your life over your relationship with God.**

_____

_____

_____

_____

Maybe there are some idols in your life right now or maybe it has been years since you have put them before God. When God rescued me, I walked with Him for twenty years before He revealed to me that I still had idols in my life. I had forsaken Him, my first love and deliverer.

Revelation 2:4 says, "Yet I hold this against you: You have forsaken the love you had at first." It is easy to lose sight of WHY we do the things for the Lord, because keeping all His commandments seems such a daunting and impossible task. It is important to remember the spirit of these laws were made out of love from our Father, God, to lead Israel and ourselves into a life of practical holiness. The people could see the nature of God and his plan for how they should live through the Law.

It is so easy to make idols of things, especially when we don't understand the love that God has for us and the power he holds to keep and protect us. We hold on tightly to loved ones in hopes to attain the love, affection and support we need from them. We are also tempted to put our trust in money and possessions to protect and sustain us. In reality, it is our father God who has given all those things and not the things themselves.

When God showed me idols that I had in my life, it broke me. For me, my husband had become my idol. I was so busy serving him because I was looking for him to fulfill the things only God could fulfill. I was putting my husband in the place that God wanted in my life. I prayed, repented and worked to put the Lord first in my life, even before my husband. God then became my first love again. I remember standing in front of the mirror and for the very first time I felt beautiful because the love of my life, Jesus, fearfully and wonderfully made me. I was beautiful because he made me beautiful. I had always looked to my husband to fulfill those needs and while my husband has done his best to always make me feel beautiful, he couldn't fill the role of "Lover of my Soul" that was meant for God to fill. God truly became my first love and I found my identity in Him instead of seeking out my worth through my husband.

**Pray and ask the Lord to reveal to you some idols in your life.**

**Where are you finding your peace, your identity, and your comfort? Do these things bring you lasting joy and comfort or do you find they are temporary fixes?**

_____

_____

_____

_____

_____

_____

_____

If God has shown you some idols in your life, what is the first thing that you need to do? Read 1 John 1:9. All we need to do is confess our sin [of putting idols before him] to God and He is so faithful to forgive us. When I repented of my idol, Jesus truly became my first love and I learned to rely on Him for all my needs. When He is your first love you want to follow his ways and obey His commands because you know He loves you and wants the best for you.

# Day Three

## Talking With Him

**Start with Prayer**

Ask the Lord to bless your time together as you learn to communicate with Him.

**Read: Matthew 6:5-15**

A huge part of developing intimacy in a relationship is through communication. As humans made in the image of God we have the ability to communicate deep truths about ourselves, motivations, feelings, and values through speech and body language. Many relationships fail due to the lack of vulnerability and trust it takes to have genuine communication with another person. The same is true for our relationship with God. How can we truly get to know Him and his heart without communicating with Him?

Jesus talks a lot about how we should approach talking with God through prayer. It may seem in the passage we read that Jesus is saying never to pray in public, but let's look more closely at the context here.

Jesus starts out by saying, *"And when you pray, do not be like the hypocrites, for they love to pray standing in the synagogues and on the street corners to be seen by others. Truly I tell you, they have received their reward in full."* (Matt. 6:5) The Hypocrites wanted to be seen in order to pretend like they were righteous and obeying God's laws. They got exactly what they wanted. They were seen by everyone and the people did think that these men were more holy than the average person.

God, however, knew their hearts. If the only time we talk to Him is when we want others to see us and pretend we have a wonderful relationship with God then we are lying to others, God, and ourselves. A true relationship requires communication in public and in the privacy of our homes and hearts. When we are truly focused on God and talking with him, it won't matter what other people think. Our relationship with our true love is what matters. If you are just with God to show off to other people, that is not love and God knows our hearts. Our conversations with the Lord should be out of genuine love and worship of Him and not for the esteem and respect from other people.

**How does Jesus say God wants us to talk with Him? (Verse 6)**

_____

_____

_____

_____

Jesus goes further into teaching how we should pray by comparing our relationship with God to the other cultures around them. He says in Matthew 6:7, "*And when you pray, do not keep on babbling like pagans, for they think they will be heard because of their many words.*"

The first century Greeks and Romans believed in a pantheon of gods. The pagan worshipers believed they needed to chant repeatedly to get their god's attention because they were not always listening. If they "annoyed" the god enough, perhaps they would have their requests granted. They also believed the words they used carried some kind of magical power, so the chanting became types of incantations used to call forth their god to them.

The purpose of prayer is to communicate with our father, God, and to be real in his presence. He already sees us and knows what's on our mind and in our hearts, but loves when we talk with Him. Jesus says in verse 6, "*Then your Father, who sees…*" We don't have to chant over and over or say an incantation just right to get our God to see or hear us. He is ALWAYS listening, this is what sets Him apart from the false gods of the surrounding cultures.

So, with the trust that our loving Father and friend is already there to listen to us and even knows what we are going to say before we say it, we can come before him with confidence knowing that he will hear us (Hebrews 4:16). It's the same way you would share your day's good times and bad times with your best friend. The difference is, God has the power to answer prayers according to His will. So, we know that our prayers and conversations with God will never be in vain because we know He loves us and wants what's best for us, whether the answer is yes or no.

Biblical prayer is an act of faith, an expression of dependance on God. Meaningless repetition signifies dependence on oneself to say or act a certain way to get God's favor or attention. Through Jesus Christ we don't need to beg our God for His attention. We always have direct access to Him and He will always listen.

**What are some ways you think Christians can be guilty of meaningless repetition?**

_____

_____

_____

_____

For example, When we say the same prayer over and over and it holds no more meaning for us, like saying the same prayer at meals and bedtime. Are your words becoming more of an "incantation" or chant that you are supposed to do to receive some kind of divine favor? Do you really think about the words you are saying? Do you know what they mean?

Jesus actually teaches us how to pray, because he knew how the people had been taught by the corrupt example of the religious leaders of the day. Let's see what Jesus said about prayer and how we should approach our Heavenly Father.

**Read The Lord's Prayer in Matthew 6:9-13**

**What do you think the word "hallowed" means in verse 9?**

_____

_____

_____

_____

"Hallowed" is another word for "holy" or "set apart". When we start this way, we are coming before Yahweh and addressing Him as the one true God who is higher and set apart from all the other "gods". God's holiness is everything that sets him apart from us, the other false gods people worshiped, and all the rest of His creation.

In verse 11, Jesus prayed, _"Give us today our daily bread..."_

In Jesus' time people relied on the food they were going to eat on a day to day basis due to lack of modern storage options. This verse is asking for much more than just food, but can be referring to all our daily needs. We are in need of so many things to survive such as food, water, shelter, clothing, etc. By saying this prayer, we are acknowledging God as our provider and asking Him to continue to provide for our needs. It is more than okay to ask God for things because He loves us.

In the book of James, he talks about how many times we don't have, because we don't ask. We want to trust God as the needs arise and not necessarily in advance. We cannot plan for every need that will come, but we can know that our God is good and will always take care of us (James 4:2-3).

**What do you think the "debts" are referring to in verse 12? (Refer to Luke 11:4)**

_____

_____

_____

In Matthew's gospel, he quoted Jesus as saying, *"forgive our **debts**,"* whereas in Luke's gospel, the people he interviewed quoted Jesus as saying *"forgive our **sins**."* In this context, debts and sins are the same thing. We need our Heavenly Father to forgive us for the wrongful actions we have done and right actions we have left undone. In this way, we can come before Him dirty and leave Him cleansed by his mercy and forgiveness to go out and continue to be His reflection to the world.

When you pray this portion, it is good to pause and reflect on any debts or sins towards God and other people that may be weighing on your heart and mind.

**Do you have any debt or sin you need to ask forgiveness for right now? Feel free to confess it below.**

_____

_____

_____

_____

Take a moment and ask God to show you where you may have failed Him or others. Maybe it's a hidden action or thought that you didn't realize was a sin. Ask the Lord to reveal it to you, ask for forgiveness and repent (turn away from that sin).

In the next section, it is important to note that just as we ask for forgiveness expecting to be forgiven by our gracious Lord, we should also extend that same grace and mercy in the Lord's name to others who have wronged us.

**Why would God forgive you if you don't forgive other people? (Verses 14-15)**

_____

_____

_____

As God's children, He desires a genuine heart from us. Not just words, but also actions. In 1 John 2:9-11, He talks about loving our brothers and sisters and therefore showing that we are sons and daughters of God. Where there is no forgiveness, is there truly the love of God in our hearts? Can we truly say we are in God's family if we harbor hatred and unforgiveness towards others? How is that being a good reflection of God's love to them?

There are many stories and warnings throughout the scriptures in regards to being merciful to our fellow man, just as Christ was merciful to us. By letting the Holy Spirit move in us, giving us a gentle, kind and forgiving heart, we show the world the true nature of God. We show the world and even other believers what a loving and forgiving God we serve and that no one is too sinful or dirty for Christ's blood to cover.

**Is there someone who has sinned against you that you need to forgive?**

_____

_____

_____

_____

I promise you that when you ask God to help you forgive others and to truly love them like He does, He will help you! Forgiveness doesn't mean you have to give someone who has abused you (physically, mentally, emotionally, or spiritually) access to your life. It just means when you think of them you don't harbor bitterness towards them. A past or present harmful situation can still leave scars and bring about deep emotions and trauma, but God can help you love someone who is not easy to love. Even if they have to be loved from afar. I can personally testify to this.

Lastly, Look at verse 13. Due to the phrasing, _"lead us not into temptation"_ it is easy to assume that it is God who tempts us into sin. But the context here is better said, lead us not into situations to be tempted or tested. God will never lead us into sin, however He may allow or even send us into situations where our faith and fruits of the Spirit will be tested. He wants to teach us and grow our faith in Himself. He also wants us to grow as a light for Him, and He wants us to know that we MUST rely on Him for strength at all times.

Jesus ends the prayer by acknowledging God again as the Creator and King of the universe. The one who is in control and everything in Heaven and Earth belongs to Him. Thank goodness!

**Do you have a quiet time and place to spend with the Lord daily?**

_____

_____

_____

_____

For the most part, the people we are closest to are the people we spend the most time with. But sometimes talking with the Lord who we cannot see can be hard. I wanted to have that intimacy and closeness with the Lord. I started keeping a prayer journal and before I knew it I was writing down my prayers, pouring my heart to him every day. Writing my prayers down helped me so much to stay focused because I felt like I was so distracted in my prayer life. I would be praying and then think about what I needed to get at the grocery store. Writing the prayers down really helped me to concentrate and stay focused on the Lord.

I was a busy, young, homeschooling mom with a newborn, a toddler, and a fourth grader. I started taking time everyday after lunch during the little's naptime and started digging into God's Word and writing in my prayer journal. I couldn't get enough of the scriptures. God was speaking to me and I was becoming closer to Him in a way that I never had before. It is still honestly my favorite time of day and I consider it my date time with the Lord. Oh, how wonderful it is to sit in His presence.

I encourage you to do the same! As your relationship with the Lord becomes more serious, it is important to find some time to spend with just you and Him. Let that be your challenge this week as we continue to talk about building intimacy.

# Day Four

## Hearing Him

**Start with Prayer**

Ask the Lord to open your ears so you can hear clearly what He has to say to you today.

**Read: 1 Samuel 3:1-10**

I have been asked the question so many times, "How do you know God is speaking to you?" I could probably write a whole book on my answer to this but I will try and sum it up with one Bible story.

**After reading the text, where does it say Samuel was at the beginning of the story?**

_____

_____

_____

_____

Samuel was sleeping in "the house of the Lord where the ark of God was." He was lying in the very presence of God. It was night and both he and Eli were sleeping and all was quiet when the Lord spoke to Samuel.

**Why did Samuel not recognize God's voice at first? (verse 7)**

_____

_____

_____

_____

It is important to note that Samuel, being a child, did not have the experience of a personal relationship with God like Eli did. He did not know how God spoke to his people because the visions had stopped coming to Eli during this time. When Samuel heard God calling to him, he didn't know the difference between God's voice and Eli's voice. Samuel wasn't at a place yet where he could distinguish God's voice from the rest of the world.

**Do you feel that you are at a place in your relationship with God where you know when he is speaking to you?**

_____

_____

_____

_____

**Who did Samuel ask to help him understand? (verse 8)**

_____

_____

He asked a mentor, Eli, who was more mature in his faith. Eli had disobeyed the Lord in several areas of his life, such as neglecting the spiritual and disciplinary education of his sons, but he still knew the Lord and knew His voice.

**In verse 10, what was Samuel's response to the Lord this time?**

_____

_____

_____

_____

**Why do you think Lord would speak to the young Samuel and not the more mature Eli?**

_____

_____

_____

_____

It would make sense looking on the surface that Eli would have been the one the Lord spoke to. But due to Eli's passiveness with his sons, the temple of the Lord was being defiled daily. In the previous chapter (1 Samuel 2:27-36), a prophecy was made against Eli's family due to him overlooking the terrible acts of his sons. They were defiling the Lord's house and the people and getting away with it. Eli turned a blind eye, so the Lord said he would cut off their family from being priest in His house ever again. This is why he reached out to young Samuel instead of Eli that night. Eli and his son's judgment was coming soon and Samuel was who God was going to raise up to take Eli's place as the High Priest.

**Do you think God speaks to His people today? How do we know it's God and not something else?**

_____

_____

_____

_____

One thing I know to be true is that God can speak to you in many ways. One thing to remember is that it will not contradict His Word or His character. When you read His Word make sure you don't just pull a verse out of context as justification for what you want it to say. There is honestly so much of that happening today. We have to try and read the scripture with the context it was written in mind. Who was the passage written to? What was their culture? It is important not to try and interpret the meaning of an ancient text with our modern culture and ways of thought.

Just recently, my husband and I started serving God in a whole different way. I was struggling with it at first because it wasn't how I was used to serving Him in the past. We were traveling to different churches every Sunday recruiting missionaries to come on mission trips to Brazil. I began to love serving God this way. It just looked so different from just being a pastor's wife, leading and teaching women's small groups, and serving in the local church. One Sunday, we were speaking at a church and a lady shared something out of Matthew 9:14-17. She was discussing the old wineskins and the new wineskins.

The Holy Spirit pierced my heart as she was talking, and I could not forget what He said. It kept echoing in my spirit. Later, I went to the scriptures to read and study and God made it so clear to me. He said, "Julie, the way you served me in the past will look nothing like how I will use you in the future. You will now serve me in a new way." So, for me to know it was God's voice that I was hearing, I went to the scriptures to make sure it lined up with His Word and His character.

If you feel God speaking to you or telling you to do something it will line up with scripture and His character.

**What are some things you have heard God say to you or ask you to do?**

_____

_____

_____

_____

**Did you do it or offer an excuse? If so, what are some excuses that you have given to God?**

_____

_____

_____

_____


If you feel God speaking to you or telling you to do something it will always line up with scripture and His character.

# Day Five

## A Date With God

I want today to be a day that you go on a date with the Lord. Think about it like going on a date with your Husband or friends. Here are some ideas you could do: go on a walk, go for a drive listening to worship music, go out into His creation and enjoy being with just you and Christ. Take your Bible, a journal, and some worship music. You can also write down some thoughts in the journal area below. I promise your spirit will be fed.

_____
_____
_____
_____
_____
_____
_____
_____
_____
_____
_____
_____
_____
_____
_____
_____
_____
_____

# Week Two

~

## Growing With Him

# Day One
## I Will Persevere

**Start with Prayer**

**Read: Romans 8:31-39; 8:28**

I want you to think of something that happened in your life that was extremely hard to go through. Write it below.

_____

_____

_____

_____

_____

One of the hardest times in my life was a storm in our ministry. I didn't know if I could continue to follow Christ because I felt like I couldn't move forward. I couldn't see past the storm. I remember one day, I cried out to the Lord in the shower and some verses from the book of Romans poured into my spirit. It was just what I needed to keep running the race when I didn't want to continue. I homeschool my children and one of the character traits that we learned in kindergarten was, "we don't quit; we persevere!"

I want to share these verses with you because I know as you follow the Lord there are going to be times when you just want to quit. So, my friend, I am here to encourage you as God encouraged me that day. My prayer is that if you are going through something that is very difficult, God will speak to you through these verses as well.

Read Romans 8:31 again. Write out the second question in that verse.

_____

_____

_____

_____

"If God is for us, who can be against us?" (Rom. 8:31)

In the book of Romans, Paul was speaking to the Christians who lived in Rome. He had a heart to see the believers in Rome partner with him to launch a missionary effort into Spain and other regions. There was great opposition to the gospel in Rome and the Christians were feeling the pressure. There was so much they had to sacrifice. So much they had to give up to continue following Christ. I am sure they were feeling the pressure of following Christ. As we dwell on that question, "If God is for us, who can be against us", we know that when we walk through suffering and persecution for His namesake it doesn't matter what anyone says about us. We know that God is for us, or on our side, when sometimes it seems like the whole world is against us.

I promise you in ministry, there will be times when you have to stand firm for biblical truths and it will not always be popular even among people in the church. I am a firm believer that the enemy has his people planted among God's people, I have witnessed this firsthand. So, we need to meditate on that question daily, "If God is for us, who can be against us?"

**What did God give up that was precious to Him because of His love for you? (verse 32)**

_____

_____

_____

God gave His own son to be killed because He loved us that much. He isn't going to hold back his gift of salvation to anyone who wants it. Also, if Christ gave his life for you he isn't going to turn around and condemn you. He will not hold back anything you need to live for Him and will always be on your side as you strive to follow His will.

**Looking in verse 34, who is the one who condemns?**

_____

_____

If no charge can be brought against the chosen of God, then certainly no condemnation can be brought against them either. Remember, Satan is the great accuser, but we have an advocate fighting for us.

**Who is at the right hand of God interceding for us?**

_____

_____

**Look up these verses**

**Romans 5:6-8**
**Mark 16:19**
**Hebrew 7:25, 9:25**
**1 John 2:1**

**What do they all have in common?**

_____

_____

_____

_____

These verses describe a divine advocate who continually defends God's children. Isn't it just an amazing feeling to know that Jesus is interceding for us?

**Read Romans 8:35-39**

**Is there anything that can separate us from Christ?**

_____

_____

_____

These verses are the ones that brought me so much comfort in my suffering. When Paul wrote this letter to the Romans, the church was about to undergo terrible persecution. These verses are so comforting knowing that it shows God's love for his people.

We are going to face hardships in many forms: persecution, illness, imprisonment, and even death. These things are scary and can cause us to feel abandoned by God. However, God sending his son to die for us is proof of his unstoppable love for us. He will never leave us or forsake us. Nothing can stop His constant presence with us.

**Look up Romans 8:28 and write it below**

_____

_____

_____

_____

_____

God is at work in all things. He will take what we walk through and use it for our good according to His will.

**Start with Prayer**

**Read Genesis 37, 39-41**

**Have you ever felt like you were stuck in a place and the waiting would never end?**

_____

_____

_____

_____

_____

Genesis 37 and 39 tells the story of how Joseph was sold into slavery by his brothers and through a lot of trials ended up in the Egyptian Pharaoh's prison.

**What would you be thinking or feeling if you were Joseph?**

_____

_____

_____

_____

_____

**Think about a time when you felt betrayed by someone. Have you ever ended up in an unpleasant place or circumstance that wasn't your fault. How were you feeling? Were you mad? Did you ever wonder where God was?**

_____

_____

_____

_____

_____

When the slavers bought Joseph from his brothers, Joseph had a thirty day journey through the desert, probably chained and on foot. When they finally arrived in Egypt he was sold again, like a piece of merchandise to the highest bidder.

Regardless of how he felt, Joseph did very well and was the best servant his master had. That is, until his master's wife lied about his integrity and had him sent to prison. Then in prison, he was the best prisoner that they ever had and was given more responsibilities. He assisted another prisoner in getting out of jail, but that man forgot to return the favor and help him. Would he be in prison forever?

Joseph was around 17 years old and before all these unfortunate events happened. He was a young man, probably full of pride at the dreams and promises God had given him. And now, he found himself stuck in Pharaoh's prison indefinitely.

**He was put in prison but what do you notice in verse 21 about who was with him?**

_____

_____

_____

_____

Remember Joseph was human just like us. In the Old Testament times they didn't have the gift of the indwelling Holy Spirit that New Testament believers have. The Holy Spirit would come and go. So, now what are some thoughts that you think were running through his head? He had been betrayed, sold, lied about, and thrown into prison. Joseph had definitely gone through some trials.

**Do you think those trials were changing him? Do you think God had a purpose for all these trials?**

_____

_____

_____

_____

_____


In James Ch. 1, he tells us to consider it pure joy when we face trials because the testing of our faith produces perseverance and perseverance helps us to be mature and complete, not lacking anything. I know it is not always easy to "count it joy" when we are walking through trials but those trials when we endure them make us stronger in our faith and know God in a more intimate way.

**Read Genesis Ch. 40, who does Joseph give credit to in verse 8?**

_____

_____

_____


We don't know all of Joseph's emotions or feelings. I am sure he had some of the same feelings and emotions that we have when we find ourselves in hard places. Joseph didn't let those feelings or emotions control him and he gave credit to God in every small task that he was given. Do you find yourself giving credit to God even in the small things? The fact that Joseph continued to put his hope and trust in God should be an encouragement to us. Even though he was still sitting in prison, he was giving God the glory and his attitude was focused on the hope he had in God. God turned Joseph's life around and He also sees your efforts for Him in the small tasks.

**Read Genesis 41:1-39**

**Look at verse 1. How many years had passed?**

_____

_____

Waiting is a very hard thing. Do you think Joseph ever doubted the vision God gave him about his brothers bowing down to him?

I know in my own journey of following the Lord, the waiting brought about doubt, trying to make things happen before God was ready, and etc. I haven't always had the best attitude in my waiting. Neither did the Israelites when they wandered in the desert for 40 years. There are reasons the Lord takes us on a different journey than we expect. That journey (if we let it) will help mold us into who God needs us to be.

The Lord called my husband and I into missions in 2007. We thought that meant we would just go directly overseas and start our ministry. I had no idea the path that lay ahead. It was full of twists, turns, mountain tops, and valleys. After all of these have passed, I can look back now and understand I was being molded into who Christ needed me to be.

Walking through these times was so hard, especially when God led my husband to pastor in the United States. I just didn't understand. I thought, "I didn't sign up for this," and I felt like I was in prison due to my overseas missions calling. My heart longed to be overseas and I was stuck being a pastor's wife in a country where there was a church on every corner. I didn't understand what God was doing, but now many years later it is easier to see how God used this journey. He needed me to trust and follow him, even when I didn't understand. He wanted to mold me into being more like Christ and to serve Him the way he had intended me to.

Due to all my experiences, I now have a heart for pastors and their wives. God has given me a burden for them around the world especially in the hard-to-reach places. I wouldn't have such heart for them if I would not have walked what God designed for me. I don't feel like I am in a prison for my calling anymore. I can now see the importance of what God was doing so He could use me for an important ministry that He wanted me to do for Him. It all goes back to just trusting Him and knowing that He is faithful and loves me. He knows the plans that He has for us and knows what is the best fit for us. (Jeremiah 29:11)

**Look at verse 14. Do you think Joseph had time to prepare to be taken out of prison and brought before Pharaoh to interpret his dreams?**

_____

_____

_____

_____

He had no warning yet his relationship with God was where it needed to be and God saw and was with him in everything he did. That is why we need to be ready for any opportunity by staying close to God and when he calls us up out of "our prison" we will be ready for the task.

**Who does Joseph give the credit to for introducing the dream? (Verse 16)**

_____

_____

**What does Pharaoh recognize about Joseph? (Verse 38)**

_____

_____

Do people recognize God in you when you are not in a place that you would like to be? Remember, Joseph was still in prison when Pharaoh finally heard about him.

**What happened next for Joseph? (Verse 40-41)**

_____

_____

_____

_____

_____

Joseph's journey helped mold him into who God needed him to be. Whatever situation you are in, just understand that God has a purpose for you there. Learn to serve God and others while you are waiting. He is molding you for the next task He has prepared for you.

# Day Three

## Spiritual Warfare

**Start with Prayer**

Spiritual warfare is very real and I have experienced it personally. My family was serving and ministering along the Amazon River in Brazil in summer 2023. My husband and I walked deep into the jungle to get to houses that were difficult to reach. We came to two homes that were very isolated from the village. We went into the first home and were greeted by an older woman. Her grandchildren were also there. While we were talking with the grandmother, the children went to get their father to meet us.

We shared with them that we had traveled so far because we had a very important message that we wanted to share with them. After sharing the gospel, the two children, ages ten and seventeen, gave their lives to Christ and immediately wanted to follow God in believers' baptism as their first step of obedience. The father said he was already a believer and the grandmother didn't want to have anything to do with it.

We went down to the river and my husband baptized the two children. Immediately after the last one was baptized it began to rain. It hadn't rained in months and all the villagers were worried. The boy told my husband that God must be pleased with him and brought them rain. We all ran for shelter at the father's house. He began to tell us of demons that were all around the jungle. He said they look like little children and they are very mean to the animals and when he lay in his hammock, he felt heavy pressure on him almost like he was being choked. The father said they used to worship spirits in the jungle and his mother who lives next door still does things to please them.

We told him that there is power in the name of Jesus and in His name they have to flee. We were able to teach him how to cast the demons out in the name of Jesus.

My dear reader, I just want you to understand that there is a real unseen battle going on all around us and that there is power in the name of Jesus.

**Read: Ephesians 6:10-20**

Paul is writing a letter to the Christians in Ephesus in A.D. 60 while he was a prisoner in Rome. He is telling them to be strong in the Lord. When it comes to spiritual warfare, we cannot stand alone, we need to rely on the strength that comes from the Lord. He is the one who will fight our battles.

**What are we fighting against (verse 12)?**

_____

_____

**How do we put on the full armor of God?**

_____

_____

_____

**What is the first piece of armor (verse 14)?**

_____

_____

The Belt of Truth is represented by a Roman soldier's large leather belt. It held his other weapons and kept his outer garments in place. So, to put on the belt of truth could be understood as accepting the truth of the Bible and choosing to follow it with integrity. The truth will assist in keeping the rest of your spiritual armor and weapons against the enemy in place.

**What is the next armor piece mentioned in verse 14?**

_____

_____

The Breastplate of Righteousness is represented by the metal armor in the shape of a human torso common in the Roman uniform. When we put on the breastplate, it can be understood that we are choosing not to hold on to and nurture known sin. It is striving to be like Christ and live according to his ways of righteousness.

**What is the next armor piece mentioned in verse 15?**

_____

_____

The feet are a very important part of our bodies. In short, they enable us to be mobile. The same was true for the Roman soldiers. Their leather sandals helped keep their footing and speed for battle. To put on these shoes could be understood as believing the promises of God in the Bible and counting on them to be true for you and for the rest of the world. The Shoes of the Gospel of Peace could also be a picture of our mobility in our mission for Christ.

**What is the next armor piece? (Verse 16)**

_____

_____

The Shield of Faith is represented by a Roman soldier's "tower shield." This shield was a large rectangle, able to cover their entire body. In times of a rain of enemy arrows, the soldiers could even stack these shields together and keep moving forward as if they were a giant lizard and their connected shields were impenetrable scales. The shields were sturdy enough to divert blows from swords, arrows, and spears used by the enemy. Our faith in God and His son, Jesus Christ, protects us by allowing us to reject the temptations to doubt, sin, or quit. When we are not so worried about the enemies' weapons hitting us, we can better focus on the truth and good deeds like Christ.

**What is the next piece of armor? (Verse 17)**

(Note lines)

The Helmet of Salvation is easy to picture. We can think of it as the Roman soldiers' metal protective headgear. Protecting the head is a huge priority because once the head is damaged, it would be very difficult or even impossible to keep fighting. Paul, however, was not referring to our salvation in Christ. Taking the helmet off of salvation could be understood as resting our hope in the future on Him and living in this world but keeping a kingdom mindset (look up Colossians 3:2).

**What is the last piece of armor to put on?**

_____

_____


The last part of the Roman Soldier's get-up was their main weapon: the sword. Paul refers to our spiritual weapon as The Sword of the Spirit. A soldier used the sword for offensive and defensive purposes. The sword of the Spirit is God's Word. We use the scriptures to fight off the attacks of the enemy. It's so important to hide God's Word in your heart by memorizing. Take the time to memorize scriptures, and hang them around your house where you will see them daily. Whatever you need to do to keep them present in your mind because the enemy is always ready to strike.

**What does it mean to pray on all occasions? (verse 18) Give me some examples:**

_____

_____

_____

_____

_____

_____

_____

_____

_____

_____

Here are some examples of prayer that I thought about. Pray as you go about your day. You don't have to isolate yourself from people in order to pray. You can make prayer a part of your lifestyle as you go about your day-to-day tasks for God. Talk to Him about everything. I am a big fan of spending time with Him every day and I write my prayers down because it helps me to focus better. God wants us in constant fellowship and communication with Him because he is our commander. A soldier never fights alone, and prayer is our direct line to our commander in times of strategy, need, loss, and victory.

**What does it also say in verse 18 about who we need to pray for?**

_____

_____

_____

_____

**In verses 19-20 Paul asks for prayer for who and what?**

_____

_____

_____

As we are preparing for and fighting our battles, we are to be on high alert and to always keep praying. We can constantly go to God for our own needs and our fellow soldiers in Christ as we look towards victory in Jesus!  Paul finishes his analogy by asking for prayer for himself and his ministry while in prison. He asked his fellow Christians to pray that he would have the courage to proclaim the gospel even to those in jail with him. Talk about not giving up or slowing down! Paul was always on high alert and took advantage of every opportunity to be the light of Christ and further God's kingdom.

# Day 4

## Storms In Life

**Start with Prayer**

**Read Jonah Chapter 1**

Jonah was a prophet of God who was given a mission that he didn't want to do. He chose instead to disobey God's command and run away in the opposite direction. Like Jonah, we may have commands from God in our lives that we don't want to do. Sometimes, we find ourselves wanting to run from these commands. Though there will be consequences to our disobedience, God, in his mercy, will give us another chance to serve Him when we return to Him because He loves us and wants us to be a part of His work in His world.

**In chapter 1, what kind of city does it say Nineveh was?**

_____

_____

_____

_____

Nineveh was the most important city in Assyria; the rising power in Jonah's day. Look up these verses in the book of Nahum to get a better description of the situation in Nineveh.

**List the descriptions of Nineveh in the lines below:**

49

**Nahum 1:9 -**

_____
_____
_____

**Nahum 2:12-13-**

_____
_____
_____

**Nahum 3:4-**

_____
_____
_____

Can you think of a people group or somewhere that you don't want the gospel to go to?

_____
_____
_____

List some reasons why Jonah was trying to run from what God was calling him to do.

_____
_____
_____

**Where did Jonah try to go instead of where God was telling him to go? (verse 3)**

_____

_____

_____

Some reasons why we wouldn't want to reach out to certain people groups could be: fear, stubbornness, claiming that God was asking too much, anger, prejudice, etc.

~ Lord, you know I love you, but my faith has limits.
~ I will go anywhere but _____!
~ Lord, we have people here at home that need the gospel.
~ Lord, Nineveh doesn't deserve to be saved.
~ Lord, they wouldn't listen even if I told them.

**Was Jonah's disobedience endangering the lives of those around him?**

_____

_____

_____

One huge storm we experienced in our ministry was when God was calling us to church plant in the southeast of the United States. There were already so many churches there. We did not want to serve in a place where there was already a church on every corner. We thought we could be more useful to God by going somewhere less churched.

We were told that there were not as many churches in Michigan and ended up choosing to go work with a church plant there until God showed us exactly where He wanted us to plant  The Lord did allow us to go there and we quickly found out that there actually were a lot of churches there already too. It was there that we experienced one of our biggest storms in life just like Jonah. It was not a physical storm, but one that came in the form of betrayal and lies within the church. It just about had me wanting to quit the ministry altogether.

God used that storm to get us back down to the church plant location that He needed us to be in the first place. Sometimes, God has to allow and use storms to steer us back to where we need to be because we don't want to go there willingly for different reasons. Even though God was with us the whole time, he allowed us to experience the storm so we could grow in our faith and obedience to Him.

**Where was Jonah when the storm was happening?**

_____

_____

_____

**Why do you think Jonah knew that the storm was from God?**

_____

_____

_____

The crew casts lots to find the guilty person, relying on their superstition to give them the answer. God allowed the lots to fall on Jonah. God intervened to let Jonah know that He was still there. Jonah couldn't run away so easily.

Even though Jonah disobeyed God, the pagan sailors came to know God as a result of Jonah's running away. God is bigger than our mistakes and loves all people. We can take comfort in knowing that He is in control even when we mess up. That doesn't mean that there weren't consequences for Jonah's disobedience, but God protected the bystanders so that they would see how much He loved them too.

We all must learn that we cannot always pick the mission we want to do for God. We must do our best to line up our lives with where God is working and listen for Him to tell us where to go and what to do. Mission for God is not a random mixture of our choices. It is a command to join God where He is already at work around you in your local community (Jerusalem), and he may call you to a neighboring area (Judea) and possibly a completely different country (the ends of the earth). Our obedience, however, begins with being faithful in the small things that God has given us.

**Read Jonah Chapter 2**

**In Chapter 2, was Jonah's prayer inside the fish a prayer of thanksgiving or deliverance?**

_____

_____

_____

It was a prayer of thanksgiving! It just goes to show that no matter how great our sin or the difficulty of the consequences God will hear us.

**How long was Jonah in the belly of the fish?**

_____

_____

_____

**Do you ever feel like you are running from something God is calling you to do?**

_____

_____

_____

_____

_____

_____

**Read Jonah Chapter 3**

**What was Jonah told by God to do in Chapter 3? Did the mission change?**

_____

_____

_____

_____

_____

_____

**Let's just think about this, would you want to go to a wicked city or people and be the one to proclaim destruction if they did not repent?**

_____

_____

_____

**Would that be scary?**

_____

_____

_____

**What did the Ninevites do when they heard Jonah's message?**

_____

_____

_____

The Ninevites responded by believing in God and repenting of their sins. Repentance was something that many of God's own people were unwilling to do. This was a time when God's chosen people were turning away from Him. Due to this, God began to reach out and show mercy to the pagan people who were open to God's grace. That goes to show you God's message and salvation is for ALL people, even our enemies, and He wants us to be involved in reaching them.

**Read Jonah Chapter 4**

**In chapter 4, why was Jonah so mad that God showed mercy on the Ninevites?**

_____

_____

_____

_____


**Look at Genesis 22:17-18**

**What was Israel's original purpose as a nation?**

_____

_____

_____


**In Jonah 4:3; What are some reasons that you think Jonah wanted to die?**

_____

_____

_____

There are so many different reasons why Jonah would feel that way. Maybe he wanted the people destroyed, maybe he was concerned about his own reputation, or maybe he was just mad at God for showing mercy to people he had already condemned.

Most of the time, we want judgment on the wicked or the people who have done us wrong. We don't want God to be patient and merciful except when it comes to us. We forget to see God for who He is, and how His love is far beyond what we expect.

**Look in verses 5-11, What did the Lord provide for Jonah?**

_____

_____

_____

**Why do you think he didn't judge Jonah for his defiant anger?**

_____

_____

_____

After showing extravagant mercy to the Ninevites, He then turned right around and showed that same patience and mercy towards Jonah. Even though Jonah was angry, God tenderly took care of him. If we obey God's will, He will continue to show us mercy, lead us and take care of us.

**In verse 11, who is Jonah thinking about?**

_____

_____

_____

_____

_____

When the sailors pleaded for their lives God showed them mercy. God saved Jonah from inside the belly of the fish. God also saved the people in Nineveh because they repented and turned from their evil ways. God answers the prayers of those who call upon him, and He will always work out his will. He desires that all will come to know him.

# Day Five

## A Date With God

Today think of that person or people group that you don't want to share the gospel with.

First, pray for them. Pray that God would be patient and draw them to repentance. Second, ask God what you can do to share His love and Gospel with them. Maybe it's time for just prayer or maybe it's time for action. Seek God for His will and direction in your next steps.

# Week Three

~

## Following Him

**Start With Prayer**

Once we have built more trust in our Savior by learning to listen to Him and persevering with Him through the hard times, we can start to follow Him more fearlessly and sacrificially.

When we trust God we are going to start hearing Him calling us to take action. It is our choice then to follow Him or not in what He asks. Either way, the calling may be scary. We have to be strong and brave. Let's see how God encouraged others at this stage in their relationship.

**Read Joshua Ch. 1:1-9**

**What did God ask Joshua to do?**

_____

_____

_____

God explicitly told Joshua to lead the Israelites across the Jordan River. The call to deliver God's people into the promised land was originally given to Moses. Joshua had watched Moses trust God for over 40 years, but now Moses was gone and he was the one who God was asking to complete the task. Being a new leader, I am sure Joshua was frightened.

**What was standing in the way of where God was telling Joshua to go?**

_____

_____

_____

Perhaps Joshua was old enough to have seen God part the waters of the Red Sea. But, perhaps, he wasn't. We aren't sure. What we are sure of, is that Moses reminded the people of God's power over and over again through that story. Now, Joshua was facing his own "Red Sea" in the Jordan River. Would he choose to follow God into the depths as Moses did or would he be too scared to step forward in faith?

Let's go back and look at what Joshua saw when he entered the land before. The first time, he was sent as a spy to scout out the land so that the people could be prepared once they entered.

**Read Numbers 13:26-33**

If the Israelites had listened to Joshua and Caleb many years before when God intended to give the promised land to them they would not be facing the Jordan River at this point.

**When God tells us to do something that seems crazy or scary, what does He promise? Look in Joshua 1:5.**

_____

_____

_____

**What does God tell Joshua to do in verses 6,7 and 9?**

_____

_____

_____

_____

_____

_____

**Was the task ahead going to be easy for the Israelites? Why?**

_____

_____

_____

_____

_____

_____

**What did God tell Joshua to do day and night to accomplish his task? (verses 7 and 8)?**

_____

_____

_____

_____

_____

_____

We need to spend time reading God's word if we are ever going to build a strong trust in God. Not only because of the encouragement, truth and promises we receive in God's words, but also from reading the stories of people just like us who have lived out those truths and promises.

I would like to share a story about a time God called my family and me to be strong and courageous.

God was telling us to go to China and share the Gospel and I was absolutely terrified. We were not allowed to go there as Christian missionaries because it was referred to as a "closed country". A "closed country" is one that is hostile towards Christians and the Gospel. I kept hearing God tell me over and over again through my Bible reading and his Holy Spirit that I needed to be strong and courageous. I knew that was where we were going and it was very dangerous for Christians.

When we finally traveled to China, what the Lord had planned wasn't anything I was expecting. I was mentally prepared for persecution and prison, but I had no idea what we were about to walk through. After we had been there two weeks, our 8-year-old daughter became very ill. We didn't yet speak the language, the only people we knew were two hours away.

We had to find a doctor with a translator which took some time, and she was admitted to the hospital with heart issues from an ongoing fever for about a month and severe leg pain. We were transferred to three hospitals over a month. The doctors told us the best case scenario was that she had an autoimmune disease and the worst case was that she had cancer.

We did not have international health insurance and didn't have any money for all the medical bills. In our moment of need, we prayed and stood strong trusting in the Lord to protect us, speak for us, and provide for us. God answered our prayers abundantly in the hidden Christian community around us. God healed her within a month and everything was cleared up. We are still not sure what the sickness was, but we knew that God used it to strengthen our trust in him.

**What are some "Jordan Rivers" in your way that are standing between you and the place God is telling you to go?**

_____

_____

_____

_____

_____

_____

**Start With Prayer**

Today we will explore what it looks and feels like to "Carry our cross". The Bible talks about how we should carry our cross as Jesus did, but what does that mean?

**Read Matthew 16:21-28**

**At this point, do you think the disciples really understood who Jesus was?**

_____

_____

_____

No, the disciples didn't fully understand who Jesus was at this point. They had many preconceived notions about who and what the Messiah/Christ should be. They were under Roman rule and the promises of the Old Testament said that the Messiah was going to come and set them free. The overall consensus of the Israelite people at that time assumed that meant set them free from their oppressive overlords and be given their land back. While the Old Testament does talk about the Messiah saving them in that sense, there is also a lot that needed to happen first that the Jews missed.

**Do you have any perceived notions about who Jesus is or what you think he is going to do for you?**

_____

_____

_____

_____

_____

_____

For example, Peter in one sentence declares Jesus to be the promised Messiah sent from God. That was correct and Jesus praised him for that understanding. Then as soon as Jesus began giving them the plan that he had to die, Peter's preconceived notions were challenged. Wait! You are the Messiah! You are going to destroy the Romans! You can't die! No, I won't allow it!

This is when Jesus had to step in and say, "Get behind me Satan," because he knew it was his sacrificial death that would be Satan's undoing. Simply destroying the Roman government was not going to save them from their sins. He was interested in setting them free from sin and death, not just physical oppression.

Has anyone who loved you dearly and wanted to protect you said, "Surely, God would never ask you to do that" or "God doesn't want you to face this?" Be very cautious of this person, because just like Peter they didn't have their mind on God but had it on earthly things. God will always ask us to do hard things. He knows this is how we will grow closer to him and become more like Christ. How hard do you think it was for Jesus to look at Peter and say, "I have to die. You are not able to stop it."

**I want you to think about what the cross means. Write down words that came to your mind when you think of a crucifixion.**

_____

_____

_____

_____

_____

_____

Jesus had to carry his literal death tool up a hill knowing that they were going to nail him to it. This is not anxiety. Anxiety is irrational worry. Worry is when we know something is happening or going to happen and we are fearful. Jesus was not anxious, but he was worried in the sense that he knew how hard it was going to be. The pain, the loneliness, the betrayal, but ultimately, the separation from God. He was so worried that he sweated drops of blood the night before while seeking peace from God for his mission ahead.

**What does it mean to you to pick up your cross and follow Jesus?**

_____

_____

_____

_____

_____

_____

**What is something really hard that you have had to go through for God?**

_____

_____

_____

_____

_____

_____

**Do you feel like God is calling you to something that might be very hard?**

_____

_____

_____

_____

_____

_____

**What are some reasons people give to not follow God?**

_____

_____

_____

_____

_____

**Read Matthew 10:39**

**What does it look like to lose your life for Jesus?**

_____

_____

_____

_____

_____

_____

_____

**What may He be asking you to carry in order to follow Him up the hill?**

_____

_____

_____

_____

_____

_____

There was a season that I kept hearing the Lord tell me to pick up my cross and follow Him in my daily reading and listening to God's word preached. God told my husband to resign from his position at the church we were serving in, sell our new home, and move my 16-year-old daughter from a Christian school that she loved. So, answering the call, my husband resigned his position without having a clue what we were suppose to do for income. God just told us He wanted us to further our biblical education for what He had planned for us in missions. We walked in absolute faith and trusted Him to show us where to go and what to do. To the world we looked absolutely out-of-our-minds and crazy. There is nothing easy about the cross, and there was nothing easy about what we were told to do but we just had to trust Him.

71

# Day Three
## Giving Up Our Treasures

**Start With Prayer**

Jesus gave up his life for you. This is not to say that every person is called to give up their physical lives for Christ. However, as His true follower we should all be expecting to give up our lives in a very real sense to follow Him.

**Read Matthew 19:16-20**

**Can we earn our way to heaven by being good?**

_____

_____

_____

_____

**Look up Romans 3:23 and write it down.**

_____

_____

_____

_____

_____

_____

**Read Matthew 19:21-30**

**In verse 21, what was Jesus telling the young man to do?**

_____

_____

_____

_____

**Why was this so hard for him?**

_____

_____

_____

_____

The "god" of a person's life is whatever rules his or her values, priorities, and ambitions. This god can literally be seen as their "life".

The young man's wealth captivated his heart and he could not give up "his life," his wealthy, secure life, in order to follow Jesus.

**Before we start thinking judgmental thoughts about the young man in these scriptures, is there some things in your life that you say you could not live without?**

_____

_____

_____

_____

_____

_____

_____

Why did God say that it was hard for a rich person to enter heaven? (verses 23-24)

_____

_____

_____

_____

What did the disciples ask Jesus in verse 25?

_____

_____

_____

_____

What was Jesus' response? (verse 26)

_____

_____

_____

_____

The disciples were astonished when they heard about how hard it is for a rich man to be saved. They thought if anyone could it would be the rich because they were considered blessed by God in their culture. That is why Jesus explained that with God all things are possible. Faith in Christ, not in ourselves or our riches is what counts.

What did Peter ask in verse 27?

_____

_____

**What was Jesus' answer? (verse 28)**

_____

_____

_____

_____

To follow Jesus you have to give up some part of your life and in many cases some very important parts of your life. But Jesus promises magnificent rewards are waiting for those who do this. God calls us to do hard things. And giving up anything important to us can be very difficult and sometimes painful.
Jesus had already told His followers that discipleship implied sacrifice but the reward for such sacrifice would be repayment of a hundred times as much in some form or another.

For example, if a person is rejected by his family for following Christ he will be rewarded with "fathers and mothers" and "brothers and sisters" in the family of God.

Read verse 30. What Jesus is trying to say here is that the ones we think will be so deserving of a reward will actually receive less than expected. The ones whom we might think as undeserving will prove to be first in God's eyes.

While living overseas as a missionary, I had come back to the US to visit in anticipation of our grand-daughter being born. I was staying with my daughter and her husband as we were eagerly waiting for the baby's arrival. I was struggling with the thought of living so far away as God had called us to serve Him overseas. I knew I was probably not going to be able to have a close relationship with my daughter and granddaughter because of the distance. The thought went through my head, Maybe this is just too much that you are asking to give up, Lord. That's when God said, Julie, you are not worthy to follow me if your love for them is more than me.

*"Anyone who loves their father or mother more than me is not worthy of me; anyone who loves their son or daughter more than me is not worthy of*

*me. Whoever does not take up their cross and follow me is not worthy of me. Whoever finds their life will lose it, and whoever loses their life for my sake will find it.* (Matthew 10:37-39)

**Start With Prayer**

So far, We have established that to be intimate with Christ is to grow in our trust towards Him. Then we should follow Him in his plans for the world. This means, just like Jesus carried His cross up the hill to die, as was His calling, we also will have very high, hard callings as his followers. Today, we talk about one of the hardest things that followers of yesterday, today and in the future had to and will have to endure.

**Read 1 Peter 1:6-7**

**Who do you think Peter is writing this book to?**

_____

_____

_____

_____

He was writing to Jewish Christians who were scattered all over the Roman empire and were under persecution. I want you to fully understand what they were living under. Nero was the ruler of the Roman Empire and he held parties in his gardens with the Christians' being punished as entertainment. They covered the Christians with skins of beasts, and had them torn by dogs and put on crosses. They were also doomed to the flames, hoisted up and lit on fire, to serve as a nightly illumination. Christians became the target of persecution when they refused worship the emperor as a god, and refused to worship the pantheon of other Roman gods at their pagan temples.

**Why do you think this bothered the Romans so much?**

_____

_____

_____

_____

If they didn't worship the emperor then they were viewed as atheists and traitors. When they refused to worship at pagan temples, it caused their money making business to drop. They also didn't support the Roman ideals of self power and they rejected the immorality of the pagan culture.

**In verses 6 and 7, what does suffering do for us believers?**

_____

_____

_____

_____

All believers face such trials when they let their light shine into the darkness. We must accept trials as a part of the refining process that burns our impurities and prepares us to meet Christ. Our sufferings can refine us and strengthen our faith, making us useful to God, much like a steel sword is much stronger with all the dirt and extra minerals burnt and beaten out.

**Read Philippians 3:10**
**Read Romans 8:17**
**Read 1 Peter 2:20-21**

Have you ever experienced physical or mental pain due to your relationship with Christ or for doing good things?

_____

_____

_____

_____

_____

_____

_____

Have you ever asked, "Why me?" if you have been through suffering?

_____

_____

_____

One of the prevailing attitudes in our culture today is, "I don't want any problems or any pain. I do not deserve to experience difficulties or trauma in any measure." As believers in Christ, we cannot adopt that mind-set. We are to conform to the example of Christ, the suffering servant.

**Read 2 Timothy 3:12**

**Who does it say will be persecuted?**

_____

_____

_____

Our suffering is a sign of our fellowship with the resurrected Lord who first suffered for us. We shouldn't be surprised when the world wants to hurt us or shut us up for following Christ. The darkness is always working to extinguish the flame, but the good news is that it never will no matter how much it blows. In the end, suffering becomes a sign of the glory that is to follow in our lives here on earth as well as when we enter the presence of God in Heaven.

God called us to serve the very church where I gave my life to the Lord as a young girl. I was in tears, when we went to visit and view the calling for my husband to become the senior pastor. The church was in terrible shape and I wanted to run so far away. I could've cared less if it was in Hawaii. I knew the placement was going to be hard. We soon found out that there were men in leadership positions who had adopted very sinful and evil worldviews.

Our family was on our way to be full-time missionaries in Indonesia when God said, I want you to go here instead. We surrendered to his call and went to this church even though we knew it was going to be very hard. There are so many details to share about our experience, but I will just jump forward a bit. Six months after we started serving there, we were in a meeting that felt like the crucifixion scene. I watched as the corrupt church leaders brought in a mass of people who we had never seen before to vote for their agendas.

In that meeting, I saw a demon who was manifested in a "church member". I watched them kick another local pastor off the stage and take over the meeting. They waved bi-laws from their hands saying, "This is what we go by." Which, I don't know about you, but I want to go by what the Bible says.

For two hours they picked apart my husband with total lies; half truths that were so twisted that it made me sick to my stomach. Then they asked my husband if he would compromise on the Biblical truths he stood for. My husband stood strong knowing that if he would just say yes, he would have a job, a home, and security for his family. With everything at stake, I watched my husband stand firm for the Lord. He said, "I cannot compromise on Biblical truth."

Immediately, the crowd urged to fire him. The meeting was so ungodly that that my husband looked to the few true church members that were there and said, "Let's just leave," because it wasn't suppose to be a business meeting but the leadership had turned it into one. As we all left and went into the parking lot, the corrupt leaders, their wives, and the people they brought in decided to hold a vote and fire my husband. In an instant, we lost our home, my husband's job, and our livelihood.

I want you to know that my husband is my hero in the faith and I have never met another man that has stood so strong for the Lord. Even though we had to walk through that suffering and persecution, we also saw God and his resurrection power in his provision.

# Day Five

## A Date With God

Use this page to go out in Creation and go on a date with just you and God. Just sit and spend time with Him. Draw or write on this page to describe your date.

# Week Four

~

## Continuing On

**Start With Prayer**

The book of Philippians was written by Paul while he was in prison in A.D. 61. This letter was written to the Philippian church which was made up of Gentile (non-Jewish) believers.

**Read Philippians Chapter 3**

**In verse 2, who are the dogs, builders, and mutilators of the flesh?**

_____

_____

_____

_____

Paul was very likely referring to the Judaizers as "mutilators of the flesh". The Judaizers were a sect of Jewish Christians who believed that the Gentiles had to follow the Old Testament laws, especially circumcision, in order to receive salvation from God. The Judaizers of our day are the people who say we need to complete specific works to receive salvation other than relying on the grace of God through faith in Jesus Christ. These hold on more to misguided "old law" traditions instead of faith in Christ.

Paul had the best credentials and accomplishments as a Jewish leader, but his salvation came from his faith and belief in Christ. It wasn't dependent on how fantastic a Jew he was, but by the grace of God to redeem him.

**According to verse 8, what should be our ultimate goal in life?**

_____

_____

_____

_____

**How, according to Paul, do we get to know Christ better?**

_____

_____

_____

_____

**Truly becoming close and knowing Christ will cost you! Are you willing to adjust your values and beliefs to more like Christ as you draw closer to him?**

_____

_____

_____

_____

**Are you willing to set aside time to know Christ better in your busy schedule?**

_____

_____

_____

_____

**What do you feel like you would need to give up to draw closer to Christ?**

_____

_____

_____

_____

_____

_____

We have all done things in our past and possibly present that we were ashamed of.

**Look at verse 12. What do we need to do for things that are in the past?**

_____

_____

_____

_____

**I want you to write down verse 14.**

_____

_____

_____

_____

_____

_____

_____

**In your life right now, would you be able tell someone to imitate you like you imitate Christ? Why or why not?**

_____

_____

_____

_____

_____

_____

_____

_____

**Look at verse 19. What is the mind set on?**

_____

_____

Paul not only criticized the Judaizers, but he also criticized the self-indulgent Christians. These were people in the church who claimed to be Christians, followers of Christ's teaching, but didn't live up to His model of servanthood and self sacrifice. For example, having freedom in Christ does not mean freedom to be selfish, but the freedom to be ourselves in service to Christ and others. We should take every opportunity to serve each other, just as Christ did.

There are so many times we want to quit when things get hard, especially when doubt and discouragement creep in. I have been there in my journey of homeschooling. God called me to homeschool my children in 2009 when my oldest was in 2nd grade. Every year I would ask the Lord if she could go back to school because it was so difficult. I didn't fully trust God with what He had called me to do.

When I was homeschooling all three of my children, I sometimes felt the day-to-day was more than I could bear. We had lots of amazing days where everything got done, but there were so many other days where it was hard and I had trouble seeing any fruit from my labor. I kept pressing on and fully surrendered to what God was calling me to do.

God gave me a different perspective and I began to look at school more as discipleship. I was given this beautiful chance to pour God's word into my children everyday. The Lord also blessed me to be with my youngest two children as they gave their lives to Christ.

I am now at a place in this journey where I can see the fruit of what God had called me to do. So, when God's calling is hard and you want to give up, just keep pressing forward with the strength that Christ is inside you just as Paul writes in Philippians 4:13.

**Write down Philippians 4:13 and pray it as a thanksgiving to Jesus strengthening you through the hard times.**

_____
_____
_____
_____
_____
_____
_____

# Day Two

## Healing

**Start With Prayer**

When we are physically sick we need time to heal. We also need time to heal when we are spiritually sick.

**Read James 5:13-16 and 1 Peter 5:10**

**If we are in trouble what should we do?**

_____

_____

**What should we do when we are happy?**

_____

_____

**When we are in trouble, what are some of the first things we can do besides pray?**

_____

_____

_____

_____

**When we are happy, what are some of the first things we can do besides thank God and sing praises to Him? (James 5:14)**

---
---
---
---

Let's remember James is speaking to a people group who are being persecuted and living in a foreign land.

**Look at verse 14, what does God ask us to do when we are sick?**

---
---
---

Let's look at the original wording in Greek for the sick:

Astheneõ (verb)

To be weak, feeble, to be without strength, powerless
To be weak in means, needy, poor
To be feeble, sick

Sickness in this instance included all types of bodily weakness: physically, mental, or spiritual.

**The elders were to pray and do what? (verse 14)**

---
---
---
---

In the Bible, oil is used as a symbol of the Spirit of God.

**In verse 15, what will make the sick person well?**

_____

_____

_____

For me, every time I have been spiritually sick and asked people who were stronger in the faith pray over me, I have been restored. Every single time. Not every time I've been physically sick has God healed me, but I do believe in physical healing. As I shared previously, I have seen God miraculously heal my daughter's body while we were in China. However, I can say with certainty, that every time I have been spiritually sick I have been healed.

**I want you to write down the later part of verse 16.**

_____

_____

_____

_____

**What makes a person righteous in God's eyes?**

**(Note lines)**

James says that in order for a person to be righteous in God's eyes, they have to be covered by the blood of Jesus and born again. Being obedient and living by faith are the proofs or fruits that a person has been born again. We are not saved by our works but we are saved to work.

**What is the most powerful resource we have as a follower of Christ?**

_____

_____

After my family had spent years in ministry and after the loss of my daughter I was spiritually sick. I needed healing. Spiritual healing. I started praying and asking the Lord for help. After about a week, I received a invitation from a wonderful woman in the faith to go with her to a women's leadership conference.

When we got there, we chose breakout sessions to attend. One of the breakout sessions was specifically for pastors' wives. When we walked in, my spirit was immediately drawn to the speaker. She asked everyone to share their stories, and I just sat there and listened. There was no way that I wanted to share my story. About three other ladies had shared and then the speaker looked at me and said "I want to hear your story." I was thinking, "Oh my goodness, here it goes. Are these ladies ready to hear all my broken heart wants to say?" Everything in my heart babbled out of my mouth.

After I had shared my story, the speaker expressed that she too had experienced some of the same hardships in ministry. Then I got to the part about losing my daughter and found out that she had lost a daughter in the exact same way. That woman had walked a journey like mine before me and she knew how to minister to my heart.

There were about ten other pastors' wives in that room that prayed over me. God gave the leader powerful words to pray over me that no one would have been able to unless they had walked in my shoes. I could feel my spirit starting to heal as they laid hands on me and prayed.

# Day Three
## Resting

**Start With Prayer**

Just like when you finish a long project or intense training for something, you need time to rest you body and mind. It is the same when we walk this journey with Jesus. He knows we will also need a time to rest as we grow.

**Read Matthew 11:28-30**

**Who does Christ tell to come to Him?**

_____

_____

_____

**What does He promise to give?**

_____

_____

_____

Look at verse 29. A yoke is a heavy harness that goes over the necks of ox or oxen so they can pull something such as a plow or wagon.

**What are some heavy burdens in your life that you need to give over to Christ? (verse 28)**

_____

_____

_____

When we partner with Christ and choose to follow Him there is no promise of an easy life. However, there is the promise that we can take His "yoke." A literal yoke enables oxen to work and is very burdensome. This can be seen as the heaviness of things we will go through and carry in this life. What Christ is offering is a shared yoke with the weight falling on his shoulders instead of you carrying it alone. He does this while offering us His love and peace with God as we labor for Him.

**Look up Jeremiah 6:16. What does he say about rest?**

_____

_____

_____

In Matthew 11:29, Jesus is quoting from Jeremiah.

**Fill in the verse below:**

**For my _____ is easy and my _____ is light.**

There was a time when my family needed so much rest after following God. We had had lots of redirections, hardships, the loss of a child, and exhaustion with church planting and ministry. We were tired. While we church planted, my husband worked three jobs to support us. That was hard on all of us and we were extremely tired.

Jesus made provision for his tired followers when he said, "Come

to me, all who are weary and burdened, and I will give you rest."
(Matthew 11:28) God gave us a sabbatical year in Florida. We were
still serving, but Matt, my husband, had a full-time ministry
position where he wasn't the lead pastor. Matt and I both love the
beach. It is a healing place for us. I grew up going to the beach every
year for vacation, so it always brings back sweet memories. We
spent many nights walking the beach at sunset, having picnics, and
beach time while my husband fished.  It was a beautiful time of rest
that God gave to us for a year.

**Have you had a chance to rest in the Lord? What are some ways
you have found to rest?**

_____

_____

_____

_____

_____

_____

_____

_____

_____

# Day Four
## Remembering

**Start With Prayer**

Remembering what God has done for you will help you to continue to press on in the future endeavors.

**Read Deuteronomy 8:1-20**

**In verse 1, what command is God telling Moses to give to the people?**

_____

_____

_____

**Look up Duet. 6:4-9 and write it here.**

_____

_____

_____

God is urging his people to remember all the love He has shown them through His faithfulness and miraculous deliverance. When we remember how God has been faithful is so many things of the past, it is easier to move forward in the hardships of the future. We remember that He will be with us and act for us according to His will.

**Look up Matthew 4:4. What other scripture does Jesus quote from here?**

_____

_____

_____

Many people think that the meaning of life is to satisfy all their desires here on earth.

**What are some ways people try to satisfy their lives here on earth?**

_____

_____

_____

_____

_____

_____

The true meaning of life comes from a total commitment to God and living a life devoted to Him.

**How can we live by that?**

_____

_____

_____

_____

_____

When everything is going good and you are satisfied with life do you remember to thank the Lord?

_____

_____

_____

_____

_____

_____

What does God remind us to do in Deut. 8:10-11?

_____

_____

_____

What might we be tempted to do in verse 14?

_____

_____

_____

I want you to take some time and remember all the things that God has done for you. Write down a few here.

_____

_____

_____

_____

_____

_____

_____

**What does God want you to always remember? (verse 18)**

_____

_____

_____

**If you do not remember the Lord and forget about His covenant, what will happen (verses 19-20)?**

_____

_____

_____

When I look back on my walk with Jesus so far, I still remember the rejections, loss, betrayal, suffering, and persecution. But, when I look and see how God brought me through those times and how He always walked beside me, I throw my hands up in praise and awe of Him. So, for instance when I think about how He rescued me from my sins, gave me good gifts when I didn't deserve them, took me to amazing places, provided for me, healed my daughter, and allowed me to witness my children give their lives to the Lord, I am simply overwhelmed. These are just a few of the treasures over the years that I want to store up and remember all the things He has done. Just dwelling on them helps me draw closer to Him.

# Day Five
## A Date With God

On this last day, make it a super special time with you and the Lord. Remember the things He has done during this Bible Study or even in the past. Spend some time reflecting on how you and Him can continue to grow together. Journal it here so you can keep this as a reminder for the things God has spoken to you during this study.

# Reference List

Phillips, W Gary. *The Holman Old Testament Commentary*. [Series volume number by verse]. Nashville: Broadman & Holman Publishers, 2004.

Smith, Gary, V. *The New American Commentary*. [Series volume number by verse]. Nashville: B & H Publishing Group, 2009.

Tyndale House Publisher's Inc., *NIV Life Application Study Bible* (Carol Stream: Zondervan, 2011).

Weber, Stuart. *The Holman New Testament Commentary*. [Series volume number by verse]. Nashville: Broadman & Holman Publishers, 2000.